All I have is

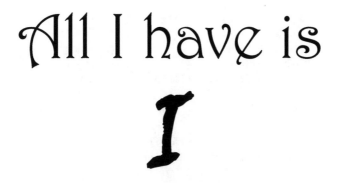

live life meaningfully!

Cannio Cardozo

WESTBOW
PRESS®
A DIVISION OF THOMAS NELSON
& ZONDERVAN

WestBow Press books may be ordered through booksellers or by contacting:

WestBow Press
A Division of Thomas Nelson & Zondervan
1663 Liberty Drive
Bloomington, IN 47403
www.westbowpress.com
844-714-3454

Because of the dynamic nature of the Internet, any web addresses or
links contained in this book may have changed since publication and
may no longer be valid. The views expressed in this work are solely those
of the author and do not necessarily reflect the views of the publisher,
and the publisher hereby disclaims any responsibility for them.

Any people depicted in stock imagery provided by Getty Images are
models, and such images are being used for illustrative purposes only.
Certain stock imagery © Getty Images.

Scripture quotations are from New Revised Standard Version Bible,
copyright © 1989 National Council of the Churches of Christ in the United
States of America. Used by permission. All rights reserved worldwide.

ISBN: 978-1-6642-1749-2 (sc)
ISBN: 978-1-6642-1750-8 (e)

Library of Congress Control Number: 2020925386

Print information available on the last page.

WestBow Press rev. date: 01/19/2021

Contents

Acknowledgment

First of all, I thank Almighty God for all the blessings he has showered upon me. I extend my thanks to Rev. Dr. Pius James D'Souza OCD (Provincial Superior of Karnataka-Goa Province) for granting the required permissions and his encouraging words. I thank Rev. Fr. Jerold D'Souza, (Provincial Delegate to Canada) for his meaningful words. I extend my gratitude to Fr. Gary Franken, Fr. Rudolf D'Souza, and Fr. Steny Mascarenhas for their continuous support and encouragement. I also take this opportunity to thank Fr. Noel D'chuna, Theresa Kennedy, Tina D'chuna, and Sharon Dilima for their genuine feedback and to my family members and friends for their prayers and wishes. At Last, I thank WestBow Press.

Foreword

If you are reading this book, I take the liberty to assume that you have had the luxury of reflecting on life, the gifts it has to offer, our existence in relation to God, and our interactions with God and ourselves. This work contains a beautiful, insightful perception of the 'self,' commonly perceived as the 'I,' and its multifarious interaction with worldly entities (which at times may comprise, if I may say so, a vicious circle). Fr. Cannio, in the wake of the pandemic presently gripping the world, has chosen to steer his time serviceably on compiling this insightful reflection—which may include his personal impressions on the meaning of life on a worldly interface viewed through the prism of involving God's gracious and grateful presence in one's life. I have good reason to believe that he has laboriously studied extensive literature on topics surrounding the subject matter of this book and simplified, for the reader, the manifestation of the 'I,' simply put as the 'Ego,' and its exhibition in wake of the varied constantly changing realities and nuances of the real world—some of which may impact us in actuality and some from a bird's eye view only, but all of which have a bearing nonetheless.

> "So we do not lose heart. Though our outer self is wasting away, our inner self is being renewed day by day. For this light momentary affliction is preparing for us an eternal weight of glory beyond all comparison, as we look not to the things that are seen but to the things that are unseen." (**2 Corinthians 4: 16–18**).

I hope you enjoy reading this deeply mindful book as much as I have, and I hope it brings to you immense joy and helps you in your introspective journey, adding to our myriad vision of life with the mercy and grace of God.

I have had the privilege of being acquainted with Fr. Cannio Cardozo, OCD, presently rendering his service at St. Edmund's Parish in North Vancouver, Canada. True to his roots from Goa, he is an enterprising and dynamic person and priest and brings much happiness, warmth, and vivacity wherever he is, be it in person or virtually. Fr. Cannio was ordained a priest in 2014, and also has to his credit a master's degree in English literature. Indeed, a man of many talents! I extend my heartfelt and sincere best-of-the-best wishes on this book and hope that you and many more people may experience its many benefits, realising that all you have is 'I' and open your hearts and minds to truly belonging to our Triune God.

—Fr. Jerald D'Souza, OCD
Provincial Delegate

Foreword

This little work contains original reflections and insights of an author who was busy and engrossed in many parish ministries and activities until COVID-19 broke out. He eagerly snatched the free time and leisure provided by the lockdown to put down in writing some of his personal impressions about the meaning of life and his relationships with people and the world on one hand and the interventions of God on the other. It is a book worth reading and reflecting upon because of its investigation and exploration of a world that is wrapped up within itself.

Into this world, if and when God wishes, He mysteriously enters, and, the thoughts and the vision of the self, begin to participate in the thoughts and vision of God:

> "For my thoughts are not your thoughts, nor are your ways my ways," says the Lord, "for as the heavens are higher than the earth, so are my ways higher than your ways and my thoughts than your thoughts." (Is 55:8–9)

This happy intervention of God in apparently earthly lives can become an invasion that raises seemingly ordinary people up to the threshold of the divine.

Fr. Cannio Cardozo, OCD, hailing from Goa, was ordained a priest in 2014 and has been engaged in the promotion of vocations in Goa and subsequently in one of the busiest parishes of the Archdiocese of Bombay. In the meantime, he completed a master's degree in English literature. Now, for more than a year, he has been rendering his service at St. Edmund's Parish in North Vancouver, Canada. Everywhere he has gone, he has endeared himself to the people through his warm and joyful presence. This is his first attempt at expressing the richness of his mind in a printed book.

On behalf of the Karnataka-Goa province, I congratulate him heartily for this literary product, and I hope many more will follow. I have no doubt the readers of this little volume will be stimulated in living their lives in the world more fully and opening their minds and hearts to the interventions of God.

—Fr. Pius James D'Souza, OCD
Provincial Superior

Introduction

Human beings are the most blessed creatures on earth, having the rational power to manipulate even the environmental conditions according to their comfort. Unfortunately, though we generally function with our cognition, there are times when we act as if we are entirely ruled by impulse. What we fall short in, is the discretion of gravity of the bond between the self and the worldly entities. If it's not moderate or regulated, that means we are in the trap of entities. There is also a danger of being extravagantly rational, which can transform us into egocentric characters, which leads to a disrupted relationship with other human beings.

Though being primarily cognitive organisms, in times of panic, dread, and anxiety, we become irrational by functioning according to instinct. I noticed this especially during the COVID-19 pandemic; fear of death wormed its way into the global psyche, most visibly manifested in the mad rush to accumulate essential items. The height of human selfishness was reflected in the overflowing carts in the superstores. The attitude of compromise was conspicuously absent—let alone the virtue of sharing. Some were unable to imagine, and unwilling to consider, the possibility of living life on essentials. These scenes mirror an inordinate love for self, characterized by the exclusion of the other. "Is there enough for all?" was not a question considered. This is exclusively the fruit of instinct rather than rationality.

Of course, in mentioning the above events, I wish to take nothing away from the powerfully inspiring lives of the frontline workers who, through their tireless toil, pulled out all stops to cater to the needs of society by putting their own lives on the line. Many others have voluntarily gone out of their way to assist the vulnerable through exemplary acts like purchasing essentials for senior citizens, distributing free provisions to the destitute, and so on. And at this juncture, I salute all those who have lost their lives in the service of humanity during the pandemic.

Musing over these events, I was inspired to put down my thoughts and reflections, and *All I Have Is I* is the result. It deals with two aspects and is divided into two parts. The first part of three chapters deals with "I" in relation to worldly entities. Here, we acknowledge that "I" is more important than all the other entities and has the power to possess or discard any of them. A person who is aware of his or her self-worth acts based upon reason.

The second part of two chapters deals with the obsession one has with the self, which results in the breakdown of relationships due to arrogance. These chapters will also throw light on how we can liberate ourselves from this obsession. The final chapter is all about the role of divine intervention in the transformation of the individual. Every chapter culminates in a poetic summary.

I hope that you, dear reader, will find a message for life within these pages.

PART I

~

In order to be content in life, one needs to be content with what one has. Some of us may be as poor as the church rat or as rich as Croesus. What matters is whether a person is satisfied with what one has or craves more. The latter is a sign of undue attachment to temporal things.

Being content with what one has does not mean that we stop working hard to have a better life in the future. It simply means that we are satisfied with what we have at the present moment in our lives—even though they may not be the best things the world has to offer. In this first part, we will mainly focus on the mania of "this is mine, and that is mine" and the ultimate awareness that "neither this nor that can be *me*."

All things that we possess can never take the place of "I." It is very important to have full control over the self, especially concerning the things we are madly in love with. When we are tempted to over-desire or overprotect something, we should be able to think, *I should not lose my peace of mind even when I see the broken pieces of that with which I am obsessed. I should not be restless even if I don't have a particular entity that gives me comfort and security.*

This part will also throw light on how we can control our obsessions, understand our addictions in a better way, and begin getting out of them. "Minding the mind" is the best way to take control of irrational behaviors.

Let us venture forth into this journey of self-discovery.

Chapter 1

The Nativity of "I"

I have not been born according to my own accord; I was brought to life by my parents. I came with nothing except myself. I didn't have any preset notions in mind. One striking expression of this is when a child cries. The newborn baby is not crying because it is naked; it is merely a response to the instinct of hunger or pain. If the newborn had intrinsic knowledge, it would have been able to figure out that it was bare. This concept is very well understood in the discipline of philosophy called *epistemology*, which uses the Latin words tabula rasa, meaning "blank slate," to describe this state of mind.

We are born without any predefined mental content. Everything we know is learned from observation and occurrence. A newborn does not even exhibit its capabilities. Though it has the potential to be someone, it is not manifested at birth. Though we can, more or less, make out the child's potential through its genes, there is absolutely no certainty that the child will have all the traits of the parents.

Let me give my own example. In my family, my grandfather and my father were musicians by profession; my father played for the navy and for the Police band. However, I couldn't be farther from them in musical ability. Although I did do music theory, which is primarily an intellectual exercise in the initial stages, I could never keep up to the tempo when I actually had to play an instrument. The point that I want to make here is that—externally as well as internally—we carry nothing when we are born. We come to this world with empty hands and empty minds.

"I" Have to Leave

We are all sojourners bound to time and space. A day will arise when death will knock at the doors of our hearts, and they will cease beating. Oh, death! I love you the most for I need nothing to journey with you; though you don't tell me the time of my departure, you make sure that when I leave, I leave alone and with nothing. We come with nothing to the time-constrained reality of earth. The enticing world, so appealing to the eye, beguiles us with foul promises of ownership until life's last breath.

What is the message here? Let me elaborate with an example. A family was staying in a house that had beautiful architecture, but it was awfully untidy within. One fine day, the lady of the house worked around the clock, cleaning and tidying up. After a long day, she went to bed just to relax for a while. She left a note on the door that read, "Do not disturb."

Her school-going son came home in the late afternoon, and to his surprise, the house was spick-and-span. Various thoughts crossed his mind. He doubted whether he had entered the right house. His eyes started to hunt for his mom to inquire about the drastic change in the house. He had no clue where his mom was until he found the note on the door.

Unwilling to disturb his resting mom, he ventured to wash up and change. Usually, he'd fling his shoes and socks all around and then have to hunt for them in the morning. He'd leave his bag open on the sofa with his books strewn all over the place, as if everyone in the house were studying them. His ironed uniform would be found crumpled up under the dining table. His disorder matched the disorder the house was already in. However, today was different. The house was different, and so was he.

Unwilling to disrupt the order his mom had so painstakingly set, he ventured to be orderly himself. He neatly placed his shoes on the shoe rack, and his bag found its way to its rightful place in the closet, along with his uniform. He was a different person today. The hours passed by, and the man of the house arrived. He was wonderstruck by the neat and tidy house.

He knew beyond a shadow of a doubt that it was his wife's work. He assumed she must be having some friends over, but he couldn't fathom who these extraordinary friends could be to be deserving of such a grand preparation. His better judgment suggested that he retain the arrangement in the house. His usual habit was to barge into the house tired and hungry, rush to the kitchen to grab a cup of coffee and something to eat, and proceed to watch TV, plonked on the sofa with his legs resting on a teapoy. Instead, he went to his room and placed his belongings in the proper place. After a wash, he made a snack for himself without leaving a mess in the kitchen and proceeded to have it with his coffee without dropping crumbs all over the sofa. The new order of the house had gotten him and changed him too.

Eventually, the lady came to the living room after her rest. She expected to see a mess again since she knew her husband and son would be home by then, but she was pleasantly surprised to find the order in the house intact.

When her husband saw her, the first question that jumped out from his mouth was, "What's special today?"

Her answer was very realistic. Standing in the middle of the living room, connecting the eyes and the hands to the existing environment, she said, "This was the ideal state planned for our house when it was interiorly designed: everything in its respective place."

It is essential to maintain the designated order of things. Order begets order—just as chaos begets chaos. The ideal truth of life in this world is whatever takes birth into the world is mortal. That is the environment in which we live. Due to our own comforts, we fail to keep the mark and live as if there is no end here on earth. As in the story, we notice that the lady put the house in order, which resulted in the husband and the son becoming conscious of the order of the immediate environment, leading them to evaluate their own dealings with it and to adapt accordingly.

Just as both of them were aware of the environment and maintained the discipline, we need to be aware that life ends with death and live accordingly by not being attached to the things that take us nowhere. And very often, our comforts and pleasures, enjoyments and indulgences, steer us away from this truth and toward an illusion of timelessness, which inadvertently blinds us to the ordered cycle of created things—whatever takes birth into the world has an end.

To maintain the order in the given situation is essential. A distortion of the due order of created entities results in diminishing or enhancing of their value, which is expressed in negative and degrading characteristics, like selfishness and greed. Living a selfish, greedy life will not take us anywhere; we will only lose our identities and value among the temporal things, and at last, it will be too late to find ourselves. Hence, we all have to be wise and alert enough to understand the worth of entities around us and adapt accordingly. It is said that the wise man learns from the mistakes of others. Let us be wise and move on to our destinies—being not carefree but careful. What is the difference? Let me elaborate with an example.

Imagine your child is fast asleep in a pin-drop silent room. When you enter that room, will you create a loud noise and be insensitive toward your child? No! Obviously, you will be very wary of your child who is in deep sleep. Most people would probably walk on their tiptoes to fetch the thing they need in the room. Similarly, we should be aware of the veracity around us, and this stresses the actuality that we all are in the realm of passing reality. This realization should imprint in us the truth that you and I will definitely have to say goodbye to this life-giving and life-ending world. "For life and death are one, even as the river and the sea are one," says Kahlil Gibran.

Once there was a young man who smoked like a chimney and was occasionally drugged to the eyeballs. He got fed up with this habit of his and wanted to get rid of it. However, he was helplessly addicted. After every experience of being as high as a kite, he would think, *Let me give up this behavior.* He would make endless promises, but he would never keep them. He was born with a silver spoon, and deep down, he was a sensitive person. One fine day, he thought of renouncing everything to live an ascetic life. He visited a monk and narrated his tragic story. He also mentioned that his best friend was the cause of his degraded state of life. His friend, who was a regular in painting the town red, showed his true colors when the addiction took over. He finally realized that this "friend" was more interested in his affluence than being there for him. With his heart open and tears in his eyes, the young man confessed to the monk that he wanted nothing more to do with these false friends and false pleasures.

The monk realized that this young man wanted to run away from life rather than face it, and after listening patiently to what he had to say, he began walking toward the edge of the cliff that overlooked the sea with the young man at his side. He pointed to a ship in the distance that had recently left the harbor. The monk turned to him and said, "The ship docked at the harbor is, without a doubt, safe, but that is not what a ship is designed for. Your purpose in this life is not to remain safe by renouncing everything; it is not the solution to the problem. You have been blessed with an abundance of wealth and a plethora of abilities. These are not to be cast aside but used for your growth and the good of others."

The monk invited him to walk with him and took him to the bank of the ocean. He pointed to another ship that had recently left the comfortable harbor and had proceeded toward its voyage in the rough, endless blue ocean. He said, "Being encircled by the deep blue waters, the ship doesn't sink, but if water seeps into the ship, then it is in danger of sinking. Similarly, you are surrounded by wealth and all the attractions that the world can offer. Yet, these things can cause you no harm, unless you become attached to them."

It is true that we are born with nothing; however, that does not mean we should own nothing as well. We cannot run away from things because they might ruin our lives. The ship requires the water to move on in its journey, and we require the things around us to go on living and growing. The way we engage with them is what marks the difference between growth and ruin.

The world is a beautiful place to live. We come to the world filled with a variety of material stuff. Naturally, we have to be a part of it; there's no doubt about it. We all are unique and interdependent. At the same time, we should imprint on our minds that this world is not permanent. Everything that takes birth has to die—one day or another.

"Death is not the opposite of life, but a part of it," says Haruki Murakami. Death puts a full stop to our earthly lives, and if we start to forget this fact, we will be vulnerable to forming attachments because we will live under the fantasy of permanency of all things, and consequently, the necessity and urge to acquire as many of them as possible.

This reminds me of an incident that took place in a philosophy class. The professor asked the students, "Can you tell something that you are absolutely certain of in life?"

One of the students ventured a reply: "I am absolutely certain that after your lecture, I will go straight home."

The professor disagreed, saying, "There are many possibilities. Your friends may invite you for a bite, and you may land up in the canteen sharing your friend's joy or on the playground, or you may visit the washroom before you go home. We don't know what is in store for us at the very next moment."

Another lad stood up and spoke about his soccer match,

affirming that he will certainly be playing at the soccer field in the next hour.

The professor replied that in this case, there could also be myriad probabilities. The opponents may not come, resulting in a walkover, or the coach could decide that you play in the second half.

After a few other such replies and counter-replies, the professor stated, "The one and only certain thing in life is death. We may not be informed of the time and or the date, but its existence in the life of every person is absolutely certain."

The nativity of "I" here on earth always contains the clause: "I have to leave." A prominent element in this is how I have lived my life. I can't be negligent of the fact that I am growing as I am gearing into every new day of my life. When I reach the peak of my physical growth, it discontinues at one point, and then the energy begins to diminish.

At my deathbed, before my demise, what remains is "I." All the worldly affluence and pleasures will not be next to my cot to revive me in the last moments of my life. In the Holy Bible, Job says, "Naked I came from my mother's womb and naked shall I return. The Lord gave and the Lord has taken away; blessed be the name of the Lord" (Job 1:21).

GONE WITH NOTHING

With nothing to something, I came;
I was dressed and named
By some other names.
I was taught and brought up;
Never did they give up.
And as I grew old,
More could I hold.
I realized it late, but not in waste,
Holding all this was a waste.
All I own is in vain,
To leave it all here, a pain.
What can I do, with no option,
But to leave behind every possession?
With nothing, I came to something,
And from something, I shall be gone with nothing.

Chapter 2

~

I Am Precious

Once and Not Twice

We are only born once. This chance given to us is not repeated. Life, enveloped in the experiences and abilities of our bodies, is the substance, the underlining principle, of our existence. Everyone has a different approach to life. Some perceive it as a precious pearl; they tend to handle their bodies with kid gloves. A number of people see life as a pain in the neck and are not bothered about their physical well-being.

Life has always to be prized in our worldviews. Just look at any distillation process; as the content is being heated, the vapor that is emitted is directed through the ice water that transforms into the appropriate essence. Though the essence is in the content, at the end of the procedure, the separated essence is more valuable. Similarly, life is encased in the body invisible to the naked eye, but it plays the vital role of animating the body. The spiritual term for this animating essence is the *soul*. If it leaves the body as the vapor does, it will take away the very essence of the body. Life is important, but at the same time, the body has to be taken care of too. If it stops functioning, life cannot be retained.

To be born into an aristocratic family is a blessing, and only a few are fortunate to be from such blue-blooded clans. The large majority of people are from the working class. Many of these people, with their talents and hard work, have excelled and passed from modest abodes to bungalows and mansions. Surely, all progress in life is to be encouraged. However, we must remember that everything natural or artificial is a gift given to us; we have not come into existence with any of this.

People with whom we move and the talents we possess are not from our accord; it is all due to Divine intervention. In the bargain of owning worldly belongings, we should always keep in mind that all that we possess and what we are today will all pass away one day because nothing is permanent. In the beginning, we feel excited to own something, but the interest in that thing slowly diminishes. That is a positive sign, but when you are in the moment of excitement of owning an object and if some kind of accident takes place with regard to that thing, in that situation, if you are able to stay calm and say, "It's okay—it is not a permanent thing," then hats off to you.

Let me share one of my experiences. It was the early 1990s, and I was in a single-digit grade. To have a refrigerator in a middle-class family in those days was one of the greatest assets. We didn't enjoy that privilege yet, but I would always imagine that if we had a refrigerator, I would drink chilled water all the time and play pranks on my brother by sneaking behind him and dropping ice down his T-shirt. When I would be full after consuming the same type of food cooked by my mother, I would keep the remaining food in it and save myself from my mom's whacking for wasting the food.

Ice candy would be on the top of my list of new things to try making, and if it didn't turn out well, I could try tricking my sister into tasting it and having a good laugh. Thinking of the diverse range of milkshakes and juices chilling in the refrigerator would have chased away all kinds of lethargy before studies and before games. Colorful jellies and other delicious desserts would have been nested in my refrigerator for the guests and friends.

In that year, all this was like nailing jelly to the wall because we were facing a financial crisis. A couple of years later, we bought a refrigerator. It was brought in as a queen, and I had a meticulous consideration to enthrone her. I burned the midnight oil to go through the catalogue thoroughly and learned how to make the utmost use of the queen of our house.

In the beginning, I was nutty as a fruitcake, overprotecting it, especially when my cousins would come for vacation. I was like a boulder protecting and guarding it. A scratch on it was equal to a wound on my flesh. My affection was that strong. A slight bang while shutting the door was like a loud blow on my eardrum, such was my concern for it. As the years passed by, my bonding went on diminishing, and at last, my interest led to the dogs. However, as its novelty waned with the passing months, so did my interest, until it became to me what it was always meant to be: an appliance used for a specific purpose.

It is, of course, natural to be excited over new things that come into our possession, but it is always good to make a conscious effort to refrain from being obsessed with things. Imagine how excellent it would be if we be calm and unruffled at the sudden damage or loss of a "branded" possession of ours. Though I was just a child, the above experience makes me realize that my obsession with man-made objects can sometimes be greater than my interest in the God who made me.

Sincere introspection will reveal that a lot of our worry and anxiety is due to the tendency to give more attention to the temporary commodities of life. We are unreasonably disturbed if they are lost, mishandled, or destroyed. Worrying on temporary commodities that has no enduring guarantee is like carrying coals to Newcastle.

Saint Teresa of Avila, one of the doctors of the Catholic Church, said, "Let nothing disturb you. Let nothing frighten you. All things are passing away. God never changes. Patience obtains all things. Whoever has God, lacks nothing. God alone suffices."

As the years go by, the material things, being temporary by

nature, eventually become obsolete. Here, let us remind ourselves of the paradox of antiques. The older they get, the more their value to admirers increases, when ironically, their usefulness and relevance to practical life decreases.

Radhanath Swami said, "Don't take this material world so seriously because it is always changing. Something terrible that you take so seriously today is going to change tomorrow."

It is very evident that there is a drastic change in the modern world. For instance, from Alexander Graham Bell's phone to the latest iPhone and from Thomas Edison's bulb to LED bulbs, there is a day-and-night difference. An Indian sage, Tirumalai Krishnamacharya, says, "Knowing all objects to be impermanent, let not their contact blind you; resolve again and again to be aware of the self that is permanent." Life itself deserves a prime place. What is the use of all things to us if we no more have life itself?

Hard work bears fruits for the individual who toils day and night. When we utilize our God-given talents, it brings success to our lives. It is good to have possessions and positions, but to have attachment to them is dire. It is good to possess things, but it is not good to be possessed by them. Attachment toward any inorganic or nonliving being is not healthy for content and serene life. Even if we possess the most precious artefacts, we should live as if we do not own them.

There is an anecdote of the taro plant. A lot of people prepare a side dish out of its roots, but the interesting fact is that, the leaves of this plant can contain the water without allowing it to get wet. This plant usually blooms in tropical areas during the monsoon season, and if parents dig for the roots, the children hunt for the biggest leaf to play by holding the water. Life, in a way, should be like the leaf that allows the water on it but not inside it. Sometimes, due to the strength of an attachment to a particular entity, we can feel that life itself is worthless without it.

Let me share a parable with you. In this parable, you are the protagonist—and there is no other human besides you. Imagine that you are in a cavernous desert with a blanket of scourging heat. You double up and see water far away, but when you reach it, you find that it's fake. In reality, it's a mirage.

The hasty run drains you, and now you're dead tired. In that exhausted state, you observe a few tiny scrubs with a big tree in the middle of them. Expecting the tree to be the life in the uninhabited desert, you take more steps, leaving the footmarks not on creamy wetland but on the dry creamy sand. As you are approaching the spot, your eyes are not bothered to mind the steps. They are fixed on the most outstanding tree for the fruit. When you see the first cluster of fruits popping out through the thick leaves of the tree, your eyes light up.

Without wasting much time, you rush to climb the tree. The low boughs are like icing on a cake in that weary condition. When you reach the middle of the trunk of the tree, you perceive on top of you a venomous desert snake and hand reachable fruits in its boundary. You shudder in fear, but an idea blooms in your mind. You shake the tree and pick up the fruit that falls into the shrubs and lands on the sand. The falling fruit wakes up the creatures down below. The insects that took refuge in the tree were also brought down with the force to the ground, and their flavor stimulates the taste buds to the deadly creatures beneath.

As you look down at the fruit on the ground, you notice fatal scorpions and lethal monitor lizards. Danger above and below makes your blood run cold. Now you are in a twofold creepy situation, which leads you to miss your heartbeat. You have no other option available than to hang on to the middle of the tree. In this horrifying state of affairs, when you turn back, to your surprise, you detect a web with a toxic spider. This petrifying creature starts coming closer. For a moment, you feel like you are sleeping with the fishes. At that moment, you become aware of a tiny cluster of fruit on thin branch of the tree. For a second, you forget about the world around you and stretch out your hand to fetch the fruit. This is the scenario of us when we are attached; we forget about the length of a lifetime in this world and focus on a particular object.

The understanding of this parable goes like this. The person walking is you. The climb is your journey in life. As you grow older, you become aware that you are aging, which corresponds with the snake, but you are not bothered by it because your eyes are only fixed on the fruit, which denotes your attachments. By hook or by crook, you want to have them. You make an effort to shake the fruit down. Finding them at the bottom among the poisonous creatures represents the truth that death is inevitable. No one can escape death. The approach of the deadly spider indicates the unpredictable time of your death, which doesn't come with an invitation. Despite being absolutely aware of the terrorizing situation in your neighborhood, you don't even spare the fruit on the tiny branch; this states the thickness of the bond between you and the thing you are attached to. Despite being aware of the shortness of life, we don't want to give up on some of our attachments. To end this parable, I say, "Whether we have something or don't have it, it shouldn't make any difference in life."

Our attachment can be toward a tiny object or a huge container. The fact remains the same: we are attached. Saint John of the Cross stated, "For whether it is a strong wire rope or a slender and delicate thread that holds the bird, it matters not if it really holds it fast; for until the cord be broken, the birds cannot fly." It does not matter what you use to tie the bird; the reality is the bird is tied. It does not matter what kind of affection you have or its size, the truth is that you are attached. I can't say that it's okay to be emotionally involved with the wristwatch my mom gave me as her departing gift. It appears to be a small item, but if anything happens to it, it would cause me emotional havoc. That will take place because of my irrational bond toward it.

There is a great misunderstanding between attachment and love. When you say, "I love you," it doesn't mean that I am attached to you. It simply means that whatsoever may come, I am ready to do anything for you. However, in the case of attachment, you think about your benefits and neglect the good of others.

Yasmin Mogahed offered some great advice:

> Try not to confuse attachment with love. Attachment is about fear and dependency and has more to do with a love of self than the love of another. Love without attachment is the purest love because it isn't about what others can give you because you're empty. It is about what you can give others because you're already full.

Attachment exists on a very peripheral level, and it is mostly based on beauty and attraction. Unconditional sacrifice is the underlining principle of unconditional love. I have observed many examples of unconditional sacrifice. Many parents from villages where farming is the primary occupation have toiled day and night to provide good schooling for their children so that they may have bright futures in spite of knowing that once the children are educated, they will be employed in faraway cities.

In some cases, the children have been hired by foreign companies. The parents permit this only because they love them and are ready to sacrifice their time and energy for the good of their children. At the same time, many questions arise in their minds: Who will keep up the family traditions? Who will take care of us when we are old? Who will look after the property and fields? They hold back all these questions because they want to see their children's wishes come true.

If they were attached, they would have compelled them to stay home and follow the same trade. In such circumstances, there are no options for the children other than the family occupation. In attachment, we don't like to dispatch, but we hold back that with which we are emotionally related. In love, we are ready to give away for the sake of others' well-being, and this echoes the sacrificing aspect of categorical love. By and large, parents want to see their children content and booming in life, and they may not even expect any help from them in return. Parents want their hearts to beat until they see the success of their children.

Marriages are made in heaven, but unless the couples adjust, they will not be registered in heaven. Where there is authentic love, there is adjustment. One spouse makes small or great sacrifices for the amelioration of the other spouse. In attachment, one thinks only about oneself. There is no adjustment, and what he or she does and says is final.

When a spouse is attached to the other, he or she would never allow the other to be free in communicating or interacting with others, especially with the opposite sex. Swami Vivekananda, the great social reformer of India, explained this:

> Once I had a friend, who happened to be very close to me. Once when we were resting at the rim of a swimming pool, she collected some water into her palm of her hand and stretched it in front of my eyes and said this: "You perceive this water carefully contained on my hand? It signifies Love."
>
> This was how I saw it: As long as you let your hand caringly open and tolerate it to remain there, it will always be there. However, if you attempt to shut your fingers around it and try to possess it, it will dribble through the first cracks it discovers. This is the utmost blunder that individuals do when they meet love, they try to possess it, they demand, they expect and just like the water falling out of your hand, love will retrieve from you. For love is meant to be free, you cannot change its nature. If there are people you love, allow them to be free beings.
>
> Give and don't expect.
>
> Advise, but don't order.

Ask, but never demand.

It might sound simple, but it is a lesson that may take a lifetime to truly practice. It is the secret to true love. To truly practice it, you must sincerely feel no expectations from those who you love and yet an unconditional caring.

Love encourages others to grow and bear the shortcomings of others. In love, the person is willing to receive the pain on behalf of the other. Love is divine, which can't be explained in human terms, but it can be seen in actions and felt in the depths of the heart. This is very well explained in *The Story of My Life*. Helen Keller wrote about the ways her teacher, Annie Sullivan, led her as a child, out of the dark world in which her deafness and blindness had imprisoned her:

> I remember the morning that I first asked the meaning of the word Love. This was before I knew many words (My Teacher) tried to kiss me but at that time I did not like to have any one kiss me except my mother. Miss Sullivan put her arm gently round me and spelled into my hand, I LOVE Helen. "What is love?" I asked. She drew me closer to her and said, "It is here," pointing to my heart, whose beats I was conscious of for the first time … "You cannot touch love, but you feel the sweetness that it pours into everything."

In attachment, the person is not bothered about the opinions of others. The person who is attached makes decisions for others, and when things are not going according to his or her plan, he or she is disturbed. In the case of love, the person feels for others. In attachment, one fulfills his or her wishes. "If the thing or person cannot be mine, then it cannot be anyone else's." We encounter this attitude in the attachment.

With all the uncertain circumstances of life, getting disappointed is not always the aftermath of attachment. A debacle at the eleventh hour or being disturbed by a given condition are not always because of attachment. To explicate this point, let me share an incident. I know a qualified professor at one of the renowned colleges in India. He wilfully renounced his teaching career in order to join the religious life and profess the evangelical vows. From the stated options, he decided to answer his divine call by accepting the religious brotherhood and not the priesthood.

At the outset, it was quite challenging for him to understand the bonafide implications of giving up worldly possessions and positions. Gradually, he discovered his divine mission. As a religious brother, it was achievable for him since he was well equipped intellectually. His mission was to assist the teachers in knowing the young minds of their students and to help the students discover their strengths and create goals.

To highlight his other aspect of life, he was also called to share his spiritual knowledge with the various parishes in order to catechize the faithful. Shouldering these kinds of responsibilities frequently led him to churches and high schools. He embraced the life of a pauper, which he affirmed through the vow of poverty. We all expected him to live a life of detachment, and he was trying his best to live accordingly. He told me about an incident when he was invited to one of the higher secondary schools to conduct a seminar on parenting for the students and parents. He had taken his brand-new laptop, which his brother had gifted him, and while he was setting up for the session, he was told to plug the cord in a socket that had no grounding system. As a result, the laptop was burned inside and stopped functioning.

He said, "That was the apt time to test my patience. At that very moment, I was upset and nervous because I had nothing written down to carry on the conference. For a while, I was in quandary and didn't know what would happen next. I called the teacher and asked her to lend me a pen and a paper to jot down whatever points I had in my mind. By the grace of God, I did exceptionally well.

"I was not upset because of the socket that damaged the laptop, but the situation was such that I had to remain calm. I was not worried about the laptop, but for a moment, I felt helpless without the laptop."

Once he returned home, he was not disturbed about ruining the laptop, but he was happy that everything went well by the grace of the Almighty. Though he mentioned the mishap, he was calm while narrating the incident. As we see here, we have to take into consideration the context to understand the gravity of attachment.

Life is a farrago of attachments and detachments. Obviously, love is the most expected thing, and you are prone to get attached to persons, places, and possessions. These are meant for a definite phase in life, but after that, you should know how to let go and embrace new things. The world is beautiful, and you have to believe in it. When we let go, we create room for something better.

One of the most content minutes in life is when you find the audacity to let go of what you cannot amend. To turn a blind eye to uncomfortable occurrences of life on account of others' faults is a blessing in disguise. Whether we live alone or in a family, we all are under the umbrella of some kind of community. It can be colleagues at a job, club buddies, worship group, a circle of friends, or an organization. They make you part of a community. Therefore, we all share an interactive interdependence with each other. This will surely arise during heated arguments and quarrels. When unpleasant situations take place, we tend to hold grudges against the offender and look for opportunities to take revenge. In order to live a colorful life, we have to let go of all types of hurt feelings. When you let go, you detach yourself and make room for new experiences in life.

The example of this religious brother takes us further into the understanding of attachments. Being committed to a goal and being industrious in your efforts to achieve it should not be mistaken for attachment. In other words, aiming at a goal is not an attachment.

First of all, we have to realize that we all are unique; there is no other you. We all have different goals to achieve and various dreams to be fulfilled. It is crucial to have a purpose in life, and these goals and dreams motivate us to make our lives more meaningful. Most of the renowned personalities in various fields are known to have pursued huge goals and seemingly unfathomable dreams in life.

Goals and dreams are essential, but if someone is not able to accomplish them due to unavoidable or unexpected circumstances—and if this leads to disappointment and a loss of hope—it can be an indication of an unhealthy attachment. Aim for the moon, and you will be among the stars. We have to burn the candle at both ends, but if we are not successful, we should not be heartbroken because there is always room in life for another goal.

Many ambitious young men and women enter depression when they fall short of achieving their goals. This can happen in any field—and in education or employment. Letting go of the past to take a step into the future with renewed vigor is the hallmark of detachment.

Michael Jordan said, "I can accept failure—everyone fails at something—but I can't accept not trying."

A comedian cracked a joke, and the audience laughed and applauded. He cracked the same joke again, and only few responded. The third time he cracked the same joke, not a soul in the hall reacted. At the end of the joke, he said, "Dear friends, you all did not respond in the same way to the same joke repeated thrice. Similarly, we have to respond to our failures of not achieving our goals in life wherein we should not ponder on the same failure now and then. On the contrary, we react all the time in the same way to our failures and wish to be in a broken state. We have to move on in life—even if we have not fulfilled our dreams. We may be compelled to give up on our goals and dreams, but we should never give up on life because every cloud has a silver lining."

Nelson Mandela said, "The greatest glory in living lies not in every falling—but in rising every time we fall."

Our God-given talents can boost our popularity. We all are the carriers of the diverse composition of DNA that identifies our uniqueness. We all have different talent levels, and that's the beauty in diversity. Our talents are always given to share with others. If we don't share them, they won't be known.

Many people get attached to their own talents. Whenever we are attached to our talents, we hesitate to share them with others. Allow me to share an incident that took place in my seminary life. Seminary life is different from normal family life. Once in a blue moon, we were allowed to go home. The rest of the days, other than vacations, we were expected to reside in the seminary.

The seminary used to host a big annual event for benefactors, well-wishers, and the parents of the seminarians. That year, the entertainment team decided to stage an opera. In order to stage an opera, there is a need for a variety of artists, singers, actors, musicians, directors, writers, dancers, and backstage handlers.

Our seminarians were really gifted in their particular fields. Many of them were proud of their faculties. When the practices were scheduled, a handful of them would deliberately appear half an hour late just to confirm to others that they had vital roles. Everyone's involvement was according to their whims and fancies. At the same time, the performance was round the corner, and there was a lack of time.

The behavior of the artists was brought to the notice of the reverend incharge, and he called a gathering of the seminarians. While we assembled in the hall, the reverend approached with a bucket of water. Some seminarians thought it was time for indoor games and imagined embarking on a rollercoaster. Others were perplexed and thought, *How come he's carrying the bucket? He could have told one of us. That means something is fishy.*

He commenced his address with a smile from ear to ear, and then he identified a muscular individual who was well-known for the regularity of his workouts. He asked him to carry the bucket of water with one finger for twelve meters. Right at the start, he thought it was child's play. He was confident, but after a few steps, his finger strained. As a result, he put down the bucket.

The reverend called him back and told him to use two fingers. Having total trust in himself, he held it. When the weight of the bucket felt heavier and heavier, he halted midway.

For the final round, the reverend told him to use all his fingers. For a brawny person like him, it was like shooting fish in a barrel.

The reverend said, "All of you are very talented, but if we don't use them, what is the use of us having them. If you believe that one of you can make a great difference to the opera, then imagine how much difference it will make if all of you come together as one team. Be humble and make use of your God-given gifts. Don't be attached to them so much that you fail to share them for the common good. As with one finger, he could not accomplish the given task. Likewise, we won't be able to have success on the appointed day. With all the fingers moving in tandem, it was possible and easy to do the task. Similarly, we all have to come together—leaving behind our differences—and work as one team."

The motivating words of the reverend encouraged us to go the extra mile. One of us was the salt of the earth, and without any selfish motives, he used to play the guitar and sing in the refectory for birthdays. He was not bothered about whether the others were listening or not, but he knew for sure that the birthday boy was enjoying.

In my close friend's case, he was always excited to act, and he was so attached to it. He used to wait in the wings for the role of the protagonist. We all are gifted in one or another. Let us not be like a donkey who praises his own tail. We should be like the lamb. Even if we are not appreciated for our talents, the talents always remain with you.

If we feel bad in a situation, it's a clear sign of attachment. The person who is attached to his or her gift will seek glory and will be full of jealousy against the others. This person will have pride to the core. Many people assume that beauty is their quality, and they imagine that they are one of the celestial bodies walking in the sky. Saint Augustine said, "It was pride that changed angels into devils, it is humility that makes men angels." When we are possessed by our potential, pride creeps in and gives us the false hope of eternal popularity.

Attachment leads to selfishness and self-centeredness. Money is the root cause of evil, especially when we are selfish. When we fail to think about others, we don't forget to think about money. To explicate this, let us take an incident that took place during the time of COVID-19, the infectious disease caused by a newly discovered coronavirus. This contagious virus spread like wildfire, and people were dropping like flies. Since millions of people were ill—and thousands of them kicked the bucket—the WHO declared this coronavirus a pandemic. As a result, there was a lockdown around the globe, which led to the downfall of the global economy.

During this world crisis, a migrant family moved to a new rental house. The owner of the house was rich beyond the dream of avarice. He owned four or five other homes in the prime location of the city, but he was still greedy. The poor family had two kids and three elders who had promised to pay him by check every month.

The man was upset and worried about whether they would be able to pay the rent in the midst of an economic disaster. He started pestering the family to pay in cash because he was skeptical about banks. He intended to hoard cash in order to feel the money every moment and seek security in the money.

During that time of horror in the world, people needed to help one another. A majority of citizens were not helping others. If the house owner had showed mercy upon that family and exempted them from only one month's rent, they would have imprinted his compassionate face in their hearts and minds. Had he been poor, it would have been a different story.

Due to his profound attachment toward money, he failed to be magnanimous. I remember the tears rolling down from her tiny Mongolian eyes as she asked me how to answer the children when they asked why they didn't have a permanent house as their friends did. Why was their food quantity and quality reduced after staying in that house? Why did they notice their dad and mom tense and worried? She was unable to face the bitter reality. That pathetic condition of that family took place just because of greed.

Out of his abundance, the rich man was not generous enough to reach out to the poor. Success is not about how much money you make; it's about the difference you can make in people's lives.

I am precious, and then I seek. In the frantic search to make ends meet, we slog around the clock. I urge you to stop and smell the roses. We should keep in mind that we are more precious than all the worldly belongings. We must be watchful of the possessions we seek to have at any cost. Life is not always about accumulating; it is about stopping and reflecting on what makes you go insane and what really and truly matters.

I wish to end this chapter with the immortal words of Jesus: "For where your treasure is, there will your heart be also" (Luke 12:34).

OH, WORLD

Oh, world! In you, I am
But called to be apart from you.
All you have, you bestowed on me.
All that you presented, fashioned me.
Though all was not eternal.
I thought it was, and offered my all.
Alas! What fashioned me, enslaved me,
And I lost all of me.
It all happened for I loved,
But love never schooled me to possess.
When I let go one by one what fashioned me,
All I gained was newness all around me.
When I suffered the pinch of slavery,
I came into my senses and unfastened my fist.
That disciplined me, and I learned to let go.
Oh, world! Now I know
What to own and what to leave.
Now I own and am not owned.

Chapter 3

~

All Goes in Mind

The Mind Minds the Brain

In order to free ourselves from our attachments, it is very important to understand how the mind works because most of our attachments are not in the physical body. They rest in the mind. To get the ball rolling, I started digging into the word *mind*. To my amazement, I learned about the vast inconsistency in the understanding of the words *mind* and *brain*. At the same time, there is a great correspondence between these two entities, and they almost appear to be two sides of the same coin. This investigation obliges me to throw light on these two words for a better understanding of the terms.

There is an extensive tradition in philosophy, religion, psychology, and cognitive science about what constitutes a mind and its distinguishing properties. All these disciplines have overlapping perceptions, but philosophy and cognitive science have highly rational classical arguments. The relationship between the brain and the mind is one of the essential questions in the account of philosophy, and it is a tricky dilemma, both philosophically and scientifically. The distinct philosophical schools like *dualism, materialism,* and *idealism* hold different opinions of the given question. Dualism holds that the mind is autonomous, existing independently of the brain.

Materialism supposes that mental phenomena are indistinguishable to neuronal phenomena. Idealism states that only mental observable facts exist. They consider the mind somehow nonphysical.

Neuroscientists don't reject the mind chat for casual conversation, but they mainly insist that we don't relate the mind as if it is actual or distinct from the brain. They reject the idea that the mind has an existence independent of the brain. To those of us without knowledge of neurobiology, it seems completely natural to refer to the mind. We say, "I am emotionally attached," "That makes me think," "It reminds me of that thing," or "I am dreaming of you." These are examples of "mind conversations." There is no actual involvement of the brain with regard to the collection of data through the senses.

Now let us have a short glimpse of the anatomy of the brain. The brain is an element of the body's central nervous system. It is a pliable mass of supportive tissues and nerves linked to the spinal cord. It is the most complex portion of the body, and it has the ability to transmit and obtain a massive amount of information. It integrates sensory information, and it controls autonomic functions such as heartbeat and respiration, while also coordinating and directing correlated motor responses. Even doctors and scientists have a hard time trying to understand the complexity of the human brain.

At this juncture, let me highlight some properties of the mind. One of the dictionaries states that the mind is that element that enables a person to be aware of the world and his or her own experiences of thinking and feeling; it is the faculty of consciousness and thought. It also includes imagination, perception, judgment, and language, and it is housed in the brain. It is responsible for processing feelings and emotions, resulting in attitudes and actions.

According to various sources, the brain and the mind are not the same. The brain is a part of the perceptible, tangible world of the body. The mind is a part of the imperceptible, transcendent world of thought, feeling, outlook, conviction, and fantasy. The brain is very much connected with the mind and consciousness, but the mind is not restricted to the brain. It has a marvelous influence over all bodily systems.

To justify the clear-cut distinction between the brain and the mind—the details of which have been dodging neurologists, scientists, philosophers, and psychologists for years—I would love to mention some points from *What Makes You Tick* by Dr. Gerard Verschuuren:

- Brain waves are material. They can be small or large, short or long. They can be measured and quantified. Thoughts are immaterial. They can be true or false or right or wrong, but they can never be small or large or heavy or light. They are unquantifiable.
- Neural activity is not necessary for mental activity. There may be mental activity even when there is little or no neural activity. Examples include near-death experiences and out-of-body experiences.
- The same thought can be transported by the different vehicles of language, actions, expressions, and gestures.

The human brain is the most complex organ in the body. Scientists have taken years to understand the human brain and do not yet comprehend it totally. The brain and the mind are the two different entities—one physical and the other metaphysical respectively—but they are interdependent. The brain is the visible element, and the mind is the invisible element, exclusively found in the human body. Consider the example of light. The light that we witness with our naked eyes is the visible light; it is the electromagnetic radiation within the realm of the electromagnetic spectrum that can be perceived by human eyes. It is just a small segment of the electromagnetic spectrum.

As a whole, the electromagnetic spectrum consists of gamma rays, x-rays, ultraviolet rays, visual light rays, infrared rays, microwaves, and radio waves. Significantly more than half of the reality of light can't be perceived by the naked eye, yet that which is invisible does exist. We can't comprehend the reality with our human vision, but that does not mean it does not exist. Similarly, since we can't perceive the mind, that doesn't mean it doesn't exist. Another example would be that of air, which consists of a major portion of nitrogen followed by oxygen and a little number of other gases like carbon dioxide and argon. We can't see air, but with the help of scientific apparatus, we can investigate its features. Likewise, we can't perceive the mind, but with the help of psychological experiments, we can know its features like thought, judgment, emotions, and fantasies.

The purpose of elaborating on the word *mind* is to help comprehend the categorical relation between the brain and the mind, which will hopefully strengthen our resolve to reject all kinds of temptations toward attachments that arise in our minds through the faculties of the brain and the five senses. For instance, the mechanism of the olfactory system, which is controlled by the brain, can lead a person to olfactory temptations. The sense of smell and the sense of taste are part of the chemosensory system; they are the chemical senses because they detect chemicals in the surroundings.

Smell works at a radically larger distance than taste does. When we inhale deeply, the air is absorbed into our nostrils over thin ridges called turbinates; this air, cleared by the nasal hair, passes the olfactory sensory neurons, which are found in a small patch of tissue, high within the nose. Glomeruli accumulates signals from these receptors and transmits them to the olfactory bulbs. Each olfactory neuron has one odor receptor. Atomic molecules released by the stuff surrounding us, whether it is fish or garlic, stimulate these receptors. Once the neurons detect the molecules, they send messages to the brain, which recognizes the odor. These representations are registered by the brain as specific smells.

In this whole process, the identification of the particular smell takes place in the brain. Similarly, the final result is attained by the brain with regard to all the senses. Sensory neurons send information from the eyes, ears, nose, tongue, and skin to the brain. Motor neurons carry messages away from the brain to the rest of the body. When a message arrives in the brain from anywhere in the body, the brain tells the body how to respond. For example, when a spark falls on your arm, it discharges a message of pain to the brain. The brain then transmits a message back informing the muscles in your arm to pull away. This process takes place in a fraction of a second.

Senses are transducers from the physical world to the domain of the mind where we interpret the information where our perceptions of the reality around us are shaped. The information that the brain accumulates is applied in day-to-day life by the mind. When we are attached to the given information of a particular entity, the mind reminds us that all that shines is not gold. The mind helps us decide on our attachments.

Yongey Mingyur Rinpoche said, "Happiness and unhappiness are not primarily created by the material world or the physical body. First and foremost, they are decisions of the mind."

BRAIN TO MIND

Numerous are dumbfounded at the mystery of the brain.
Several are confounded to know where the mind lies in the brain.

There is rain in the brain,
Poured by senses quicker than the bullet train.

There is a breeze in the mind,
Blown by the divine, which no one can find.

If the brain is a mass of a complex chain,
Then the mind is abstract and can train.

Even if we are enticed by the sensory brain,
The mind decides what is gain and what is pain.

Mind your mind

Experts state that the mind receives between fifty thousand and seventy thousand thoughts per day. Practically speaking, though these occur in the mind, the latter has no control over them. The mind can't decipher what the next thought will be. The thoughts continue emerging from time to time. By way of illustration, think about when you are praying or thinking about future plans. As you are totally involved and absorbed in this particular activity, you suddenly notice that your thoughts jump like a monkey from one tree to another. They jump from the focus on God in prayer to something else in the world. While you are thinking of your future endeavors, you will suddenly find yourself racking your brain on an irrelevant topic that is far different from the future undertaking you were contemplating. That is why we have several individuals complaining that they can't pray because they get distracted or can't concentrate on just one thing because their minds go haywire.

It is quite evident that the mind is in the driver's seat of the human body, monitoring the conversion of thought into behavior. In other words, the mind has the ability to make decisions by choosing the thought to be put into practice. Let us take the case of our thoughts. They may be positive or negative, encouraging or discouraging, yet we can't act upon all of them. For example, if the thought of having ample money pops into your mind, you will not put it into action by robbing a bank. It is obvious that you will think about whether it is right or wrong. This entire decision-making process takes place in the mind.

The mind has the aptitude for making a deliberate effort to think about a specific entity or concept. For instance, as I am writing this, I make a deliberate attempt to think about the topic I am writing about. The mind also acts as a rudder, leading the emotions within a regulated space. For example, at some point in our lives, we might have felt down in the dumps. In that pathetic condition, a few of us might have gone to the extent of generating the thought of ending life. In these types of miserable situations, the mind constantly tells us that after every sad day, there is always a bright day. Even in terms of happiness, the mind must have always warned us, now and then, about overexcitement and overconfidence. Though emotions can blind the mind due to the alluring reality presented by the brain, the mind has to eventually pay for it with regret for any wrong decisions.

In this magnificent world, we can't help but admire the uniqueness of everything within it. The order and the system in nature are mind-blowing. At the same time, we can't forget the discoveries and inventions achieved by human beings. Often, the diverse things of this world are very appealing to our senses, and we seek to find pleasure in them. With the help of our human faculties, it is not wrong to derive pleasure from the natural and artificial entities in the world. However, we should always remember that truth is relative. What is true for one may not be true for the other, and that which is good for one could be poison for another. Glucose is good for a child serving as a source of energy to the body, but for a person who is diagnosed with diabetes, it is considered a poison. Similarly, what is pleasurable for one may not be pleasurable for others. Plato said, "Beauty lies in the eye of the beholder." This is a fitting statement to describe the relativity of our subjective judgment. When, with the help of our brain, we accumulate a wealth of information from the outside world, the mind is often tempted to plunge into it. At the same time, the mind does have the ability to pause, analyze, and, if necessary, say no to the negative information it is drawn to.

Various fascinating natural and man-made things exist for temporal admiration and not for eternal intimacy. The beguiling realities around us belie this truth. We remain in an illusion that everything that glitters is gold. Sometimes, we are blinded, lost in the darkness, and not able to understand what is to be done. For example, having a crush on someone is normal to human nature. Feeling upset and restless about not seeing the crush—let's say,

Carol—every day is not objectively real. It is good to look at Carol's beauty as a refreshing factor in the present—but not as a permanent measure of beauty in the future. If the mind is not instructed, one will be lost in daydreaming about Carol. Gradually, the thought that one can't survive without her forms, in the mind, choking it to such an extent that there is no place for any other thought to sustain.

This is also the experience for many people who have been ditched by a significant other. It becomes a tough fight for them to get over such an experience, and tragically, some succumb to the beguiling thought of life not being worth living anymore. If you have undergone this kind of situation in your life, what was your reaction? Did you cry bitterly all day and every day? Did you listen to your mind telling you that ups and downs are a part and parcel of life—and it will go by in a few days?

I should continue much more sturdily in pursuit of my dreams instead of dwelling on this gloomy situation. I helped one of my friends get through a similar situation. When he looks back now, he laughs at himself for being so foolish in his perception of reality. Every stunning beauty has to be admired along with the belief that the future will bring something even more astonishing.

There is a great chance of attachment when the mind zeroes down on a particular entity. It could be alcohol, social media, drugs, money, fashion, cosmetics, porn, or a relationship. When our thoughts revolve around this one thing, the mind eventually starts prompting actions toward attaining it by hook or by crook. Yet, we aren't animals; we have the power to reason out and make decisions that are good for us.

When we find ourselves totally drawn to one specific entity, it is absolutely necessary to make a deliberate effort to focus the mind on something besides what you are addicted to make the mind think about something besides the petty obsession that is magnified by our thinking patterns. For example, in the moment of temptation, we can talk to a friend or turn to a hobby. There are amazing things around us that can draw the mind away from contemplating substance abuse, lust, or wealth. We have to listen to our thoughts and evaluate them from time to time. Look for any thought patterns or emotions that seem to be impacting your daily life. If we fail to keep an eye on our thoughts, we can be led toward self-destruction.

We all are aware of an inner voice that provides an ongoing dialogue in our minds, and this is known as self-talk. These internal monologues can be positive or negative. The positive voice within us is very important to tear down fear and raise the curtains of confidence. Human nature is vulnerable to negative self-talk; that's why many people with low self-esteem say, "I can't do it" or "I am a big failure."

Generally, people consider self-talk as something that is not within a person's control. These disorganized pieces of information pop in and out of the brain at the drop of a hat. However, if we analyze it, we realize that we have a lot of control over self-talk—and it starts by being conscious of what we are saying to ourselves. We can't guess what conversations will develop in our minds, but we can become aware of how internal dialogue has a significant impact on our lives.

The cognitive outbreak in the mid-1900s brought out the consequence of thinking in the human experience. Psychotherapists Albert Ellis and Aaron Beck made a great contribution, and the world came to know the importance of thinking in our lives. Prior to this, behaviorism prevailed in the psychological realm, and attention was given to understanding the impact of our thinking on our behavior. Cognition and behavior are dependent upon each other. We are not to be lost in negative self-talk. Bob Proctor said, "Don't be a victim of negative self-talk."

Self-talk is a vital instrument in controlling our attachments. When we are aware of our obsessions and are struggling to do away with them, we need the assistance of self-talk. With its aid, we can command our minds to examine our own behavior and the objects we are preoccupied with.

Whenever turbulence takes place in the mind as a result of the clash of a contradictory attraction, we need to ask ourselves certain questions: Do I really need it? Can I live without it? Have I not lived many happy years without it? Do I require it so much? These and many more questions are based on what is good and right for us.

We need to be content with the self-talk. Take a look around the house. There will be numerous things we don't use. We find excuses not to discard them—like the clothes and shoes stacked neatly in the closet, which we may have not used for a long time—and find it difficult or painful to give them away.

With the lockdown measures imposed during the time of the coronavirus pandemic, many people have become aware that they can actually live well enough with less. When we find the urge to purchase stuff that may not be that urgent, it is always beneficial to stop and ask ourselves if we really need it. Do we truly require that much of it?

A woman explained how she became aware of her obsession. She was infatuated with buying expensive trinkets, thinking it was her hobby. Due to this misconception, she would buy any novel trinket without a second thought about the cost. Though it was a humiliating matter to articulate, still she gathered some courage and said, "My nine-year-old son opened my eyes. When my son asked me for money to enhance his stamp collection, I refused. He hesitantly said, 'What about my hobby?' At that very instant, I understood that a hobby would never cost an arm and a leg since it is the best way of utilizing leisure time at a minimum cost. This so-called hobby had turned into an irresistible habit."

Today, she says, "I constantly have self-talk while shopping, especially when I notice a fascinating trinket. In this mania of mine, I even informed the dealers to keep the item for me. I told them I would collect it the next day, and I was aware that my tomorrow would never come. That's how I slowly and steadily won over my bad habit. It was all possible because of my self-talk."

A number of times, others have guided us back to the right track when we have been lost in our attachments. Though they influence our thoughts, it is up to us to amend our lives. It is like taking a horse to the pond; we can't force it to drink water. Our loved ones can just direct us, but they can't compel us. Between spouses, it happens in the form of mutual correction, and in the case of the children, it takes the shape of parental guidance.

This reflection reminds me of an elderly religious brother who lived in the bosom of the mountains of Anaheim Lake in British Colombia. His life was a reflection of simple living and high thinking. He was the salt of the earth, and he rendered his religious service for the Native Indians. He was content and as calm as a cucumber, and he was blessed with the patience of a saint.

Once or twice every couple of months, I used to visit that place for three days to help him with the religious services. During those three days, my dwelling was the brother's tiny house with minimum households. On one of my visits, the brother and I thought of going for a sunset stroll. As we were stepping into the woods, out of the blue we noticed a patch of mushrooms beside the narrow path. I was thrilled! I had only heard about the mushrooms of Anaheim Lake, and now I was witnessing them with my own eyes.

As we were collecting them, he abruptly stopped and said, "This is sufficient."

I thought he was kidding. *Who would leave something that is free—and the best of the lot?* Turning a deaf ear to him, I continued to uproot some more.

He again asked me to stop.

I said, "Why? It will last for a week if we collect them all and store them."

With a compassionate smile, he looked at what we had, and said, "This is *need*." He pointed to those that were still growing beside the path and said, "And that is *greed*."

In that moment, he helped me say no to my desire to possess. Our loved ones play a great role in influencing us and helping us control our obsessions. When someone goes out of their way to do so, the least we can do is pause and reflect on the merits of their advice.

The common advice of parents is to not play with fire or water. Many times, we act like fools and think, *I will play with these for a while, but I will remain in control.* When I think a little is okay, that little becomes a little more. It turns to be the reason for my distraction. That little more is like the tip of the iceberg; no one knows if it will drown us.

My dad is in his golden years, and it has been fifteen years since he last touched alcohol. Years before, he would be on cloud nine at the sight of whiskey or rum. When he was employed in the naval band, in those glorious days of his life, booze was like his second wife. He was able to purchase it at a subsidized rate from the naval canteen.

At most of the socials, my mom used to keep an eye on him because he used to have a whale of a time with his friends and his drinks. She knew very well that anything more than two pegs was going beyond his limit. To control his excitement, she would constantly be around him with a watchful eye. He was warned by her, now and then, before he would get drunk.

He usually said, "I just started; it has not even touched my throat." He was smart enough to deceive her with his made-up taradiddle. This desire for a little, and then a little more, would eventually get him drunk. After the party, he would be with his bottle for three or four days without moderation. Other than those few days, he would be sober.

By and large, he was a family man. Today, he is altogether a different person. He is grateful to God for giving him the grace to quit his addiction. When he was asked how it was possible, his reply was modest and unambiguous: "I went within myself and analyzed my thoughts, especially those that would lead me to drink without proportion. I found out that the root cause of it all was my erroneous thinking that a little was okay. To avoid that, I began to say to myself, 'A little is not okay.' Whenever I was tempted to drink hard alcohol, I would plunge into a drink of lesser strength, such as wine or beer. Gradually, by the grace of the Almighty, I could overcome my obsession."

We have a great lesson to learn from him. When we are addicted to something, do not say, "A little is okay." This applies to those who are addicted and for those who have control over their actions—but it is a different story in their case. If we can't handle the fire, it is better not to play with it.

The mind is responsible for our behavior. In order to have self-control, we need to discipline ourselves by training our minds. "You either control your mind or it controls you," says Napoleon Hill. Always remember that too much is too bad. The very fact that we become too close to something or someone is the sign that we are going out of control. Instead of saying, "A little more is okay," we need to say, "It is not okay—enough is enough."

When we can stop, we don't want to, and when we want to, we can't. That is the reality of addiction. Keep an eye on your urges before they get worst. We need to divert our energy in a constructive way; in the beginning, it may appear useless, but in the long run, the effort will reap a bountiful harvest. Whether we are young or old, we all require a reason to live, a purpose that builds us. As a youngster, focus on career, and as an elder, cultivate simple hobbies. It is important to keep yourself busy.

What goes, goes in mind. We often complain about our senses and say that they are the cause of our addictions. As we have seen in the first part of this chapter, the job of the senses is to transmit the message from the world outside to the brain; it is the mind that longs and seeks the object of attraction again and again. We need to be aware of what goes on in our minds.

Let us wind up this topic with a quote from Saint Paul:

> Finally, brothers, whatever is true, whatever is honorable, whatever is just, whatever is pure, whatever is lovely, whatever is commendable, if there is any excellence, if there is anything worthy of praise, think about these things. (Philippians 4:8)

THE MYSTERY OF THE MIND

There's constant music in the mind, but we're not
aware of the notes played when and where.
Thinking! Is that music in the mind, but we can't
be aware of all the passing thoughts.

You and I can only raise the volume of music, but
we can't change the notes being played.
We can only direct our actions, but we have
no control over all our thoughts.

When the music plays according to the notes,
a fabulous melody emerges.
Similarly, consistent effort on directing the
thoughts can bring a positive result.

Melancholic music is not played at the festivities.
Likewise, everything is not good for you—
think about what is right and best.

Musical instruments beautify the musical piece, but
the lead is played by a single instrument.
You may think everything is essential, but you
can live contentedly with fewer wants.

Music sustained on only one chord leaves out
the scope of diversity in music.
Zeroing in on one thing always brings the danger
of missing out on the other things.

Music played on multiple wavelengths brings out the best.
The monologue played in our minds leads us to the finest decisions.

Sometimes, listening to the music matters more than the lyrics.
Sometimes, listening to others and being
influenced matters more than the words.

In silence, we can hear music distinctly.
In the silence of the mind, identify the root cause of obsessive behavior.

PART II

Saint Vincent de Paul, a Catholic who was exceptional in his charity toward the poor, said: "Humility is nothing but the truth, and pride is nothing but lying."

We are all called to grow in humility and not in pride, which destroys relationships. In this part of the book, we will observe how the ego hinders interpersonal bonds. It is mostly the negative part of "I" that is reflected in the ego. The negative version of "I" is being obsessed with the self, leading to an attitude of arrogance that destroys friendships. The first chapter in this part expounds on the problem of ego. The second one serves as a guide for managing the ego.

Chapter 4

❧

Only I, Others Bye

The attitude of *All I Have Is I* is the noticeable indication of self-attachment. In the second part of this reflection, we will make an effort to understand how an overemphasis on "I" affects us. The "I" or the self is called the *ego* in Latin. Most of us are familiar with this term *ego*, which can be summarized with three words: *I, me,* and *myself.*

When we are attached to our own selves, there is no room for compromise or adjustment with others. We are pleased to float in our self-created bubble, and if somebody bursts it, we turn into the boiling bubble. A candle dispatches light, brightening the site so that it may be perceived by humans. In this entire process, it allows itself to be devoured by fire. We must be aware of this allegory.

In this entire process, the candle allows itself to be devoured by fire, and it drops down until it melts to the level. This allegory can be applied to ourselves. Unless the wick of a candle is lit, it will not be able to dispel the darkness for others. Setting a fire is like feeling the pinch of pain from an encounter with a so-called opponent—the one who bursts our bubble.

In harsh encounters, we should learn to melt the ego like wax in order to bring happiness to others' lives, keeping in mind that melted wax can be reused. We may have to melt a thousand times and stoop our heads just to save the relationship because the ego is the greatest disruptor of relationships.

I took a trip to Coorg in Karnataka, India. It was a sight to behold dressed in a sari of green foliage and adorned with coffee as ornaments. It is known for its coffee estates, and as a result, it is common to have pleasurable views of expensive cars owned by the coffee estate proprietors.

Two of my friends and I hit the road early in the morning in an ordinary car on an empty stomach. Coorg was about 180 kilometers from the place where we commenced our day's journey. By the time we arrived, it was noon. Our eyes were hunting for a decent restaurant to kill our hunger. As we were slow on our wheels, one of the most amazing cars grabbed our attention.

A friend exclaimed, "Look at that marvelous Audi!"

I had noticed the logo on the car and immediately said, "That it's Mercedes!" I said it proudly and loudly since, as a kid, I was obsessed with identify cars by their logos.

My friend started arguing and didn't want to accept what I was saying. As the argument was heating up, it brought to mind my grandma's golden words: "Does it pull off a piece of your flesh to say okay to someone who is wrong—even if you are right?"

Even when we're actually right, we lose nothing by saying, "It's fine. You are right." Many times, bowing down to an adversary or giving up is not a sign of losing; it's ages ture of victory of relationship over personal pride. Furthermore, it opens the doors to earning respect.

When my friend came to know the truth, he had high regard for me for letting him win the argument despite knowing I was in the right.

The message of salt losing taste and identity to add taste to other delicious food is also applicable to an ego tripper. If the salt is tasted before adding it in the food, it won't appeal to our taste buds. However, when it is mingled with food, its prominence is realized. Likewise, unless we dissolve the ego, we will not be able to bring the taste to the lives of others. Human beings are interdependent, and that's why all the qualities of humanity are not found in every person. Some people have more, and others have less, but by default, everyone has some qualities. This is a clear indication that we all are interdependent in terms of everyone's well-being. We should not leave the opportunity to be like salt and dissolve the ego in order to embrace others with their innate qualities. The ego is like the worm, and selfishness destroys it all. People become self-centered and grab what is due to others. Every day, I/me/myself is creeping into the lives of most of us—irrespective of social and economic status. The older you get, the more you realize that it isn't about material things or egos. It's about our hearts and who they beat for.

Flooded Pride

Let me begin with an exemplum. Many moons ago, in a small village in India, there lived a magnanimous landlord who was blessed with three pretty daughters whose unadorned appearance looked like a million dollars. He could afford to provide valuable education to all of them, but due to the social stigma against educating girls, he was helpless to do so.

He took a brave step and decided to send one of his daughters to the guru to acquire knowledge. While he was deciding which daughter was worth sending, he landed upon a tough stone to break. He decided to conduct a character test on them, and he called them all. He placed clay pots full of water on the ground, and opposite to each, he placed an empty jar. He gave his daughters an empty earthen cup and told them the rules of the game: "Do not let a single tear of the cup kiss the ground" and "More the life, worth the jar." The understanding of this rule is that, not a single drop of water should fall on the ground while taking the earthen cup. The more water you collect in the jar is much better.

He told them to take the water from the pot to the jar in

their respective cups in one round. The first daughter, who was overconfident, filled the cup until the brim, not leaving even a little space of dust. The second daughter kept in mind everything the father had said. Understating her limitations, she filled it a few millimeters below the brim. The younger daughter thinks that if she fills a little more than half, she will definitely spill the water. Felling low of herself she takes more or less half of the cup with water. In the end, all of them reached the goal. The last one reached it the first since she did not rock on the way to prevent the spill. The first one reached second by leaving her footprints on the wet mud but holding a maximum amount of water. At last, the second one was seen near the jar. Though she was last, she was announced as the winner.

This was a bitter lesson for the elder daughter. She started to seek justification, hammering the fact that she had gathered more water in the jar. She believed she was the winner.

The father said, "It was your pride that failed you. You thought you knew everything and understood everything. The 'the tear of the cup' means you were reckless when you handled the cup. As a result, the water dropped out of it like the tears of those who you handle harshly, mainly because of your pride. The people living around us deserve respect and concern. You were not bothered about the water falling out, and in the same way, you are not bothered by others' feelings while handling them. You filled it to the brim, thinking that you are capable of everything, and you were overconfident about your abilities."

The younger daughter was sitting at the corner and did not even whisper a word.

The father turned to her with compassion and said, "I know you have not spilled a single drop, and on top of that, you were the first to finish the target. Due to your low self-esteem, you poured less water in the cup. As a consequence, you brought less life in the jar. This is the reason you are not the winner. It is not a lack of capability or opportunity that keeps you back; it is simply a lack of confidence in yourself."

The first daughter often said, "I know everything," "I am the best," "What do you know?" "I know better," and "Why should I listen to you?"

We should take pride in how far we've come and have faith in how far we can go. As a consequence, people often say, "I am proud of myself" or "I am proud of my son." These are positive expressions. It's a good sign to have a positive outlook.

The second daughter was confident—but not overconfident. She was proud of herself—but not too proud. If your friend says that they are good for nothing and are not proud, it can lead to an inferiority complex. The younger daughter is an example of this kind of personalities. Maxwell Maltz said, "Low self-esteem is like driving through life with your hand-brake on. It is like hitting the road with fear and doubt, knowing where to go but not sure how to go."

C.S. Lewis said, "A proud man is always looking down on things and people; and of course, as long as you are looking down, you cannot see something that is above you."

It is all about looking up with wonder at the vastness of the sky and acknowledging one's nothingness below it. There is nothing wrong with being proud, but there is something wrong with letting pride reach a level that destroys relationships. In a relationship, you sometimes have to shut up, swallow your pride, and accept that you are wrong. It is not giving up; it is growing up.

We all have to strive to transcend from pride to the realm of self-acceptance in order to embrace others in their weakness and vulnerability, keeping in mind our own shortcomings. Most relationships fail because couples fight with pride more than they work with love. A drop of love is enough to make a possible adjustment in a relationship, but the truth of one's failures is hard to swallow if you are bloated with pride. William Hazlitt said, "Pride erects a little kingdom of its own, and acts as a sovereign in it."

We all have to mind our pride before it erects its kingdom; if it is not monitored, it will be hard to pull down.

You Interfere, You Fear

Individuals who are too attached to the self don't like others to interfere in their business. To shun others' interference in their weaknesses or in their undertakings, they avoid all situations that make them uncomfortable. Pointing out the mistakes of a self-centered person is like inviting unnecessary trouble. Self-attached individuals are prone to frustration since it is not easy for them to accept their own failures and mistakes. Any correction from a neighbor is like a threat to them; they look forward to seeing the "interfering" person being paid back in the same coin. These people harbor grudges and sway the net of revenge to catch their adversary at fault and prove themselves correct. It is like going about with a placard that reads: "You mess, I smash! Be careful! Don't stamp on my feet."

I spent my early years living in a minor seminary. Whenever there was a tussle among the players on the soccer field, my colleague would say, "Today we are here; tomorrow we will be somewhere else. Let us resolve it here and not keep any anger."

I now realize how right he was. No matter how hard we try, we will never get together as a group again because we are all scattered across the world. When we were together all those years ago, it was common to express our anger by saying, "Let me see you on the playing field."

The last-benchers were more interested in sports than studies. The front-benchers were no saints either; they would publicly put the not-so-smart ones down. It was almost like a competition between the classroom and the playing field—and each would try to get his revenge on the other. Since both studies and games were obligatory, there was no option to escape what was coming. It all happened because nobody liked to expose their weaknesses; if someone tried to interfere, he had to be ready to face the consequences.

Most of us do not like to be corrected, but at the same time, we are not willing to realize our shortcomings and amend our ways. If we think like my wise colleague, our lives will really be a blessing to others. We have all come to this world for a few years, and no one is going to live forever—even though we may feel like we want to.

We should always think like William Shakespeare. He said, "All the world's a stage and all the men and women merely players. They have their exits and their entrances; And one man in his time plays many parts, His acts being seven ages."

All of us have to say goodbye—one day or the other—to the people in our lives and the things we possess. This fact of life should always echo in our ears, especially when we are puffed up with self-importance.

Ezra T. Benson said, "Pride is concerned with who is right; humility is concerned with what is right." We can't always be right; we know that we have been wrong several times. Only the courageous accept that they are in the wrong and acknowledge that the other is in the right.

LET ME OPEN!

When I close my eyes, I see nothing but my inner self.
When I open them, I see there is a need to pay attention to others' selves.

When I close my finger, I hold nothing but me.
When I open my fist, I hold others and say "we."

When I close my ears, I hear nothing but "I am right."
When I open my ears, I hear others and realize even they can be right.

When I close my heart, I feel nothing but "I am hurt."
When I open my heart, I feel even they have sentiments and get hurt.

When I close my mouth, I speak nothing but to my ego.
When I open my mouth, I speak to others
and allow my viewpoint to let go.

When I close my mind, I think nothing but "I am infallible."
When I open my mind, I think, *No one is perfect—and all are vulnerable.*

When I close my total self, I gain nothing but pride.
When I open my total self, I gain people and friends at my side.

Chapter 5

~

Meditate to Update

Meditation is the enormous umbrella of dissimilar practices found in diverse traditions, religions, and cultures. Such extensiveness makes it difficult to describe. According to the Cambridge dictionary, it is "the act of giving your attention to only one thing either as a religious activity or as a way of becoming calm and relaxed."

Introspection, self-reflection, self-examination, concentration, contemplation, and pondering are some of the synonyms of meditation. Halvor Eifring said, "Traditionally, meditation is strongly connected to religion. Today it is also practiced without a religious purpose, but the actual word *meditation* does, in fact, come from Christianity."

Let us have a glance at some of the major religions that hold meditation in high regard. In Hinduism, there are various disciplines and patterns of meditation. In ancient Hinduism, yoga and dhyana were pursued to attain the union of the self with the creator. This desired state is called "moksha."

Buddhism, on the contrary, doesn't contain belief in a God, but meditation is a prominent activity in their religion. The goal of Buddhism is self-realization or "Nirvana," and meditation becomes the vehicle to attain this enlightenment. Jainism also doesn't propose a belief in any personal god, but they have a concept called "Divine."

The individual who liberates himself or herself from the cycle of birth and death and attains lasting happiness becomes another Divine. This emancipation can only be attained through meditation or dhyana, and this state of the soul, completely free from the cycle of reincarnation, is called "Nirvana."

In Christianity, meditation is mostly used as a form of prayer to connect to God and to ponder on the Word of God, which reflects in one's daily life. In the Catholic and Orthodox traditions, many of the desert fathers and hermits were spending time in solitude in order to attain union with the Almighty.

As a whole, Islamic traditions don't focus on meditation, but a branch of Islam called Sufism focuses on reflection that leads to knowledge. This is attained with the help of breathing regulations and reciting secret words. Many Orthodox Jews are skeptical about the position of meditation in Judaism. At the same time, both ancient Kabbalistic and Hasidic texts support the practice of acquiring knowledge through intense rational reflection. In general, less attention is given to meditation, but the Kabbalistic sect of Judaism encourages and practices various types of meditation. In Sikhism, meditation is known as "simran," and they also emphasize the remembrance of the Word of God. According to them, these two practices help them feel God's presence and achieve union with the divine light. Thus, by and large, most of the major religions give importance to meditation to attain union with the Divine.

The same meditation, traditionally seen as an integral part of many religions, is now considered, in the modern psychological world, a mental exercise that focuses on concentration, observation, and awareness. According to contemporary studies, some of the common goals of this practice are to increase focus, reduce stress, and be mindful of one's negative emotions. The process of meditation doesn't give much importance to God. It is a hunt for inner peace and happiness without having any link to the Almighty. Primarily, meditation is based on self-reflection or self-examination, which helps a person attain calmness, leaving aside all kinds of negativity.

Thus, on the whole, for some, the end result of practicing meditation is inner peace and enlightenment; for others, it is a way to attain union with the Divine.

We all have to meditate in our own lives to keep ourselves humble and calm. Honest self-reflection opens our minds to reprogramming, transformation, achievement, and freedom. "Knowing yourself is the beginning of all wisdom," said Aristotle. It counsels even the proficient to maintain a humble profile in the realization that even they are inadequate in some aspects of life.

Meditation helps us identify our strengths and weaknesses, and it enables us to place ourselves on the right track, leading to constructive relationships. Though meditation has ample scientific benefits, such as increasing attention span, improving cognition, controlling pain, and regulating blood pressure, we are more concerned here with how it helps a person know the genuine self, leading one to a deeper understanding than the routine peripheral life. In other words, we are focusing on how meditation can make an individual a better person.

In this chapter, we are dealing with how meditation helps us understand the inner self, and it updates us about our shortcomings and failures. One of my spiritual directors gave me an example. I said, "I usually spend time meditating on the Word of God; is it also necessary to meditate on our life?"

He replied with an analogy of a fresh rose kept in a vase on the dining table. "You visit the table thrice a day for meals, and day after day, you notice that the petals of the rose are withering. You pluck them off so that the rose may look fresh and beautiful at all times. Similarly, when we reflect on the self, we come to realize the not-so-good things in us. We make an effort to pluck them off, and as a result, we become graceful and positive."

Through meditation, we can update ourselves by leaving behind our vices and motivating ourselves to practice virtues. While meditating, we come to an awareness of our weaknesses, and when any situation triggers them, we endeavor to exert control over them. Reflecting on life during meditation enables us to recognize and acknowledge our faults, particularly in situations of misunderstanding that might have led to unnecessary conflicts with those who were actually in the right.

After upsetting somebody, have you ever realized that what you had said or did was not right? Most of us regret losing our calm and creating a mountain out of a molehill. One of my friends makes a point to go for a daily evening stroll for at least half an hour whenever time permits. During his "me time," he recollects the things that went wrong that particular day. He says it is like a meditation on the self that helps him reflect on his life and reconcile with the ones he's wronged. Meditation is not a withdrawal from humankind—or from contact with the outside world—as many may think it is. It is a way of learning to understand oneself and others in order to live in peace and harmony.

The person who does meditation is like a wise person who learns from others' mistakes. Several teachers of meditation have found the virtue of humility as a result of meditation. With the help of meditation, they have come to realize that no one can be correct all the time. The one who reflects on one's life does not believe it's "my way or highway." They believe "if it's not my way, then it's your way." Ezra Taft Benson said, "Pride is concerned with who is right. Humility is concerned with what is right."

In a contemporary mind-set, meditation has been seen as a way to destress. Quite a number of contemporary forms of meditation are promoted as a "soothing balm" to get relief from the turmoil of worldly demands—in an attempt to attain mental peace. Some forms lead to a trancelike state of mind with the help of relaxing music, which behaves as a defence mechanism against anxiety. The many entities around us in this colorful world are so enticing that they disturb our concentration, easily letting the mind drift away; hence, meditation assists us in concentrating better on a particular subject.

Meditation has been considered by some as the pearl of a

healthy, physical, and mental life, helping to control blood pressure and promoting sound sleep. These benefits are among the major effects and purposes of contemporary forms of meditation, which are fair enough, but, unfortunately, they are incomplete. A good form of meditation must strike a balance between awareness practices and personality transformation, and many of these contemporary forms of meditation do not produce the rewards of self-reflection, character development, personality growth, and self-mortification. These bring about a change in a person's way of life—a "personality transformation."

We can't clap with one hand; we need the coordination of both. Similarly, these awareness practices of the contemporary outlook should go hand in hand with an emphasis on personality transformation in the acquirement of virtues and eradication of vices. In short, meditation is more than an awareness practice that helps reduce anxiety and stress, improve concentration and attention, and lead to relaxation and peace of mind. It also plays a great role in personality development. With self-reflection, it builds up good qualities like humility, forgiveness, compassion, mercy, simplicity, and detachment. Many modern meditation techniques do not take this essential aspect into account.

Almost all the giants in meditation in the course of history have spoken about the shaping of the personality. In promoting a reflection on the self, meditation annihilates the frontiers of pride in a way that builds the bond of love with others in humility and simplicity.

Many stories of simplicity and humility have been attributed to Siddhartha Gautama, the founder of Buddhism: "One who is wise and disciplined is always kind and intelligent, humble and free from pride. One like this will be praised."

The great person who established Jainism, Nataputta Mahavira, in *Marichi Bhav 3*, said, "The greater your ego, the greater your downfall." His instructions about pride and humility can be found in many other places.

One of the great Indian yogis, Mahavatar Babaji, said, "By serving both wise and ignorant sadhus, I am learning the greatest of virtues pleasing to God above all others—humility." He also said, "To humble the ego or false self is to discover one's eternal identity."

Saint John of the Cross, one of the greatest mystics of the Catholic Church, was renowned for his contemplative prayer life. He said, "To be taken with love for a soul, God does not look on its greatness, but the greatness of its humility."

Saint Augustine was a church father, a theologian, and a mystic. He said, "Do you wish to be great? Then begin by being little. Do you desire to construct a vast and lofty fabric? Think first about the foundations of humility. The higher your structure is to be, the deeper must be its foundation." In his works, like *Confessions*, Augustine speaks of traveling inward to meet God.

All these prominent persons practiced meditation in totality. As the sound of the clap is the result of clapping in the same way, some who exercised mediation in fullness call the result of meditation enlightenment (Nirvana), and others call it being one with the Divine. There is no question about what comes first since they are incorporated in to each other. We can't take just one and say, "That is meditation."

The outcome of supreme meditation is a healthy psychical state as well as an enriched personality. There is no question about which among these comes first since they are incorporated into each other. We can't take just one effect and call it meditation. An authentic form of meditation takes care of the holistic enhancement of the individual. When we genuinely meditate about life, the ego becomes melted wax, which can be fashioned in different forms and shapes. What is most essential is the realization that I am solely not the most important. I need to give importance to others as well by melting my ego and walking in humility. Meditation helps us achieve this.

MEDITATE TO BE A BETTER I, LETTING THE EGO FLY

Falling of a leaf or a petal,
What matters is falling.
Whether it's enlightenment or union with the Divine,
What matters is genuine meditation.

Leaves and petals are in a fixed position,
Letting all the whispers of birds and bees pass by.
Postured and not motioned to any place
Letting go all the taste of the senses is the spark to meditate.

Leaves sprout first in a plant,
The petals form a beautiful flower later.
Initially, to sit down to meditate is exhausting,
But later, it leads to a rejuvenating spring.

Leaves embellish a branch's cover,
Petals embroider a flower.
Awareness practice embellishes our health
Self-reflection embroiders our personality.

If only petals are intact, the flower is healthy,
But then the departure of all the leaves loses the whole beauty.
If only to meditate is to remain healthy.
But not to learn to remain with neighbors is faulty.

Leaves and petals at last both go to the ground
Some proclaim it's a fertilizer; others proclaim it's organic.
Some proclaim they are enlightened—
Others proclaim they have attained union with the Divine.

Chapter 6

~

Divine Intervention

This last chapter is the synthesis of both parts of this reflection. In the first part, we read about how an individual, "I," shows excessive interest in the entities of the world. The aftermath of this ownership, rather than "I" possessing them turns into "I" being possessed by them.

In the second part, we examined how the individual is obsessed with the ego. It is like seeking one's own well-being at the cost of weakening the bonds of a relationship. When a person attempts to turn over a new leaf and does his or her best to get rid of attachments and pride, the person is not always successful. In fact, sometimes, even with great effort, nothing works. Every endeavor seems to be in vain. At this point, divine intervention is the only solution; it brings forth the required change of life. As proof of this, there are a number of conversion stories recorded in history. We may have witnessed some people who have made radical changes in their lives, leaving behind for good their major attachments and addictions.

The transformation in a person through divine intervention may occur in two ways: direct or indirect. Direct divine intervention is mostly through some personal spiritual experience at a retreat or some other religious activity. Indirect divine intervention is like an awareness that comes through others or even through misfortune in life.

We also might have observed or heard of the personality traits acquired by individuals almost overnight: proud people becoming humble or self-centered persons turning into self-giving ones. Many of these cases can be attributed to divine intervention. What was not possible through self-reflection for many years can happen through a striking scriptural passage or through the humble and magnanimous gesture of a spiritual person. This kind of radical transformation in an individual always leads to astonishment.

When God strikes someone, he makes a totally new person out of them. It has always been a mystery to me who, when, and how God wishes to transform. Another kind of divine intervention takes place through extraordinary events like visions, apparitions, miracles, and ecstasies. These may not be exclusively for the person who undergoes them. These are considered to be indications to wake up from a slumber and amend our ways.

I would look at the impact of the Divine on an individual as a tree without a parasite. Let me explain this by taking you back to my younger days. In my backyard at home, there was a mango tree that was full of parasitic plants of the *Loranthus* family. It is a common occurrence in tropical forests, and my dad used to clear these parasites from the fruit-bearing trees. That day, it was the turn of the *Mankurad* (a mango variety) tree to be rid of its parasites.

Equipped with a sickle, my dad was ready to chop off what the young me thought was a fragile-looking shrub with supple reddish flowers. As he set his leg on the lowest branch of the tree, I rushed to tell him not to cut it off from the mango tree—for I had a soft spot for these flower-producing plants. In reply, my father told me that these were parasitic plants, and once they attach themselves to a tree, they steal the nutrients and water from it. If they are not axed off, they will hinder the growth of the host tree, and as a result, they will not produce tasty *Mankurad* mangoes. I, of course, couldn't stomach the thought of losing the chilled mango shake that my mom made with the *Mankurads* to beat the summer heat, and I was easily convinced to choose the fruits over the flowers.

In the above passage, the tree represents us with our given limitations. The parasites are our physical attachments: the craving for money and wealth, addiction to drugs and alcohol, and many more temporal goods and human beings. The parasites also refer to the incorporeal face of a person such as pride, anger, stress, greed, power, and glory.

My father was in the place of God. One day, he decided to set free the chikoo tree in front of the house. Another day, he liberated the mango tree in the backyard. The next day, he planned to clean the terminal crown of the coconut trees. And the day after that, he planned to prune the plants in the flower garden. He chose the flora to be transformed according to his choice without any indication. God also works in mysterious ways, and we have never been—and will never be—able to understand his ways of working. Today, God may choose you or me—and we may have no idea about it. Divine ways are not our ways; they always keep us in suspense.

We should rely on divine assistance for the renewal of our lives. I make all possible efforts to free myself from the dungeon of self-ruining habits and the vices that tear apart human relationships, but along with all my attempts to liberate myself, I also have faith in the grace of the Divine to help me achieve this freedom.

When we turn to God for aid, we voluntarily begin to live according to his precepts. When we walk each day keeping in mind the divine statutes, we gradually become aware of the divine presence at every moment, and this helps to sustain our efforts to overcome our shortcomings. This does not mean that we will become saints, but through this endeavor, we can at least refrain from being drawn into the clutches of our addictions.

Saint Jean Baptiste Marie Vianney is better known to English-speaking Catholics as John Vianney or simply the Curé of Ars. It is said that one fine day, he called the people of his parish around a haystack. A few meters away, a fire was started. As the people began to gather, he began to throw small handfuls of hay into the fire and say, "Please don't catch fire."

The people thought that he had gone mad and began laughing at him.

One of the prominent figures came forward and said, "Father John, obviously, when you place hay in the fire, it will burn—no matter what you say to it!"

Saint John Vianney replied, "Exactly! So also, you people send your children to parties and nights out without your presence and then expect them not to get spoiled!"

It matters a lot how we choose to nurture ourselves; if we nurture ourselves in a not-so-good environment, it will naturally affect our behavioral patterns. When we supply our minds with spiritual food, it helps us be content with what we have—and there are fewer chances of becoming attached to something. This can be seen in the lives of the saints who were involved in spiritual activities. Most of them were detached from worldly possessions, but they possessed a bundle of virtues. I try to enrich myself with spiritual music in the morning; it truly stimulates me to start my day with pure thoughts. I try to embrace each day positively, seeking to build up my life in a constructive way.

Divine intervention is the mysterious interaction of the Divine with the human. It is the hand of the Divine involved in the conversion of the individual. This type of total change is not possible in a person by his or her own accord, especially with regard to addictions and the vice of pride. However, with Divine intervention, everything is possible.

Jesus looked at the disciples and said, "With man, this is impossible, but not with God; all things are possible with God" (Mark 10:27).

THIS IS MY PRAYER TO ALMIGHTY:

Who knows all in whole, and intervenes in the
lives of some to open the eyes of many.
Lord, watch me from the threshold of
My house, until the last step of my destination.
Let love be my pen
To write the words
Of hope and comfort on the hearts
Of the people I meet.
Let your closeness bring in me,
The warmth that would drive away,
The loneliness as I roam alone.
Let your angels answer me when I am about
To encounter threats and tribulations in life.